The Bird King

an artist's notebook

Kiurun perheelle

(for the Kiuru family)

Text and illustrations copyright © 2010 by Shaun Tan

Library of Congress Cataloging-in-Publication Data
Tan, Shaun.
[Bird king and other sketches]
The bird king : an artist's notebook / Shaun Tan.
- First American edition. pages cm
ISBN 978-0-545-46513-7 (hardcover : alk. paper)
1. Tan, Shaun-Notebooks, sketchbooks, etc.
I. Tan, Shaun. Works. Selections. 2013.
II. Title.
NC994.5.T36A4 2013
741.6'4092-dc23
2012016625

Book design by Shaun Tan and Phil Falco

10 9 8 7 6 5 4 3 2 1   13 14 15 16 17

First American edition, February 2013

Printed in China   38

The Bird King
an artist's notebook

Shaun Tan

ARTHUR A. LEVINE BOOKS
AN IMPRINT OF SCHOLASTIC INC.

introduction

I'm often wary of using the word "inspiration" to introduce my work
- it sounds too much like a sun shower from the heavens, absorbed by
a passive individual enjoying an especially receptive moment. While
that may be the case on rare occasions when an idea pops into my head
for no discernible reason, the reality is usually far more prosaic.
Staring at a blank piece of paper, I can't think of anything original.
I feel utterly uninspired and unreceptive. It's the familiar malaise
of "artist's block", and in such circumstances there is only one thing
to do: Just start drawing.

The artist Paul Klee refers to this simple act as "taking a line
for a walk," an apt description of my own basic practice: allowing
the tip of a pencil to wander through the landscape of a sketchbook,
motivated by a vague impulse but hoping to find something much more
interesting along the way. Strokes, hooks, squiggles, and loops can
resolve into hills, faces, animals, machines - even abstracted
feelings - the meanings of which are often secondary to the simple
act of *making* (something young children know intuitively). Images
are not preconceived and then drawn, they are conceived *as* they are
drawn. Indeed, drawing is its own form of thinking, in the same
way birdsong is "thought about" within a bird's throat.

Klee has a second good metaphor: the artist as a tree, drawing from
a rich compost of experience - things seen, read, told, and dreamt -
in order to grow leaves, flowers, and fruit. Art, following the
laws of horticulture, can only make something out of something else;
artists do not create so much as transform. That's not to say the
process is a casual or simple one. I find that good drawing requires
conscientious effort: active research, careful observation of things
around me, ongoing experimentation and reference-gathering, all of
which exist "behind the scenes." To follow the Klee metaphor, artists
need to work hard to make sure their creative soil is well tilled and
fertilized. They need to look outward and actively accumulate a swag
of influences, things to bring along when taking that line for a walk.

While much of my work involves exhibited projects like books,
films, and finished paintings, the primary material of all these -
the compost - remains largely unseen, tucked away in folios,

boxes, and sketchbooks. Some are half-baked story ideas, either mercifully abandoned or looking for an excuse to be resurrected. Some are tests from the early or awkward middle stages of a project, very utilitarian drawings, stepping stones on the way to finished artwork. Some are exercises to simply keep fit as an artist, where the practice of drawing is about *learning to see*, a study that never ends. And then there are other sketches produced for no particular purpose at all, just for fun, and these can often be the most interesting.

The works collected here present a cross section of such material from the past twelve years, ranging from fairly precise drawings to scruffy scribbles. They reflect a spectrum of interests, starting with my familiar preoccupation with imaginary worlds and creatures, and including observational sketches of people, animals, and landscapes, which I think form the unseen backbone of all my other work. I was also interested in a spontaneity that can sometimes be missing from more finished paintings, which can suffer from excessive revision, polishing, and commercial compromise, leading to a familiar lament: "Why isn't the finished work as good as the sketch?"

I think this has something to do with the directness of small drawings, their lack of self-consciousness. Each piece in this book was generally completed in a single sitting of less than two hours, and not intended to be published at the time of execution (indeed, some have barely escaped the paper-recycling bin). Do they offer a privileged insight into the creative process? That's an interesting question for any audience, whether a general reader or a student of illustration. From an artist's point of view, at least, I think they do. There are few better expressions of the impulse to draw, an instinct that lingers from childhood, with all its absurdist daydreaming and playful seriousness.

untold stories

My stories generally begin with images rather than words, modest sketches drawn in a fairly aimless way. One of the joys of drawing is that meaning can be constantly postponed, and there is no real pressure to "say" anything special when working privately in a sketchbook. Nevertheless, interesting or profound ideas can emerge of their own accord, not so much in the form of a "message," but rather as a strangely articulated question. A scene or character seems to look back from the page and ask, "What do you make of this?" A drawing feels successful to me when it is both clear and ambiguous, something I try to underscore by adding an equally ambiguous title. While there is no set meaning in any of these drawings, there *is* an invitation to seek one (for myself as much as any other audience).

Sometimes that invitation is so enticing, it leads me to develop a longer story, as if I'm trying to find out what it's really about. Over the years, this has resulted in very complex narratives such as *The Lost Thing* and *The Arrival*, books that are full of elaborate detail and expansive themes. In many cases, however, one little drawing is enough. Free from any binding context and openly available to the reader's imagination, each sketch suggests its own "untold story."

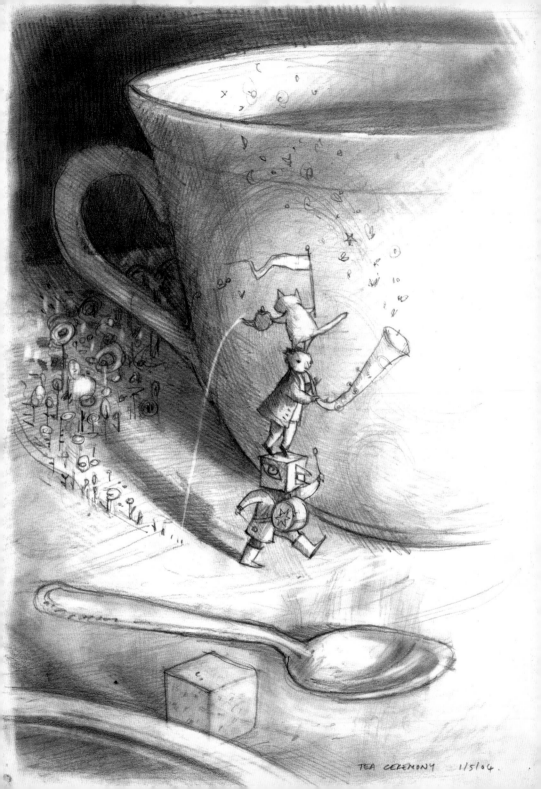

TEA CEREMONY — 1/5/04.

summoning

anthropologists

automatic teller

12

astro · artist

furnace

Neighbourhood watch

STOREY

2.00 wed

boar

17

10·50

10·20   penguin

MINIMUM UNDERSI

FIRST FLOOR MAIN

The Water Woman.

the thing in the bathroom

20

self-awareness

strawberry

ancient ones.

genesis

24

heart - bell

never lost a case

best friends

owl ghost

reading

IAN

30

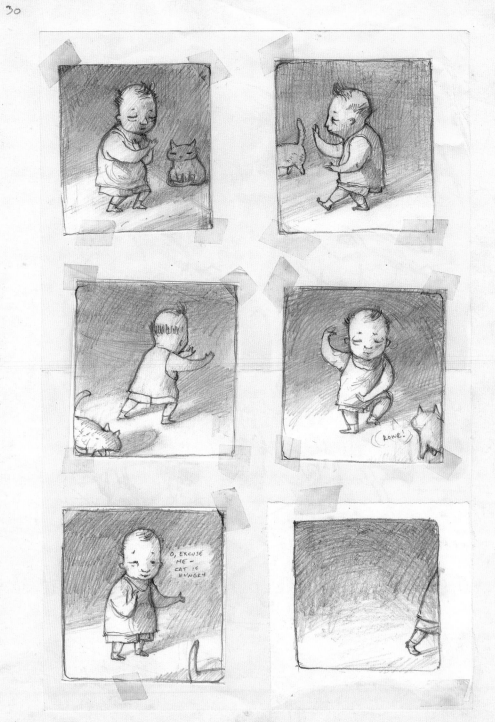

tai - chi

philbert

red donkey

summit

portrait of the artist as a young man

book, theater, and film

I've worked on many projects where production quality is critical, whether preparing an illustration for print, composing a frame in a digital film, or solving the structural problems of a puppet. Realizing a vision can be a long and complicated affair because there's so much revision and problem-solving involved, and unfortunately the original ideas that inspire a project can easily be clouded or forgotten along the way. Quick sketches are an essential means of recording some of this source energy, like pinning ephemeral butterflies to the page, a library of fresh impressions that can be used for later reference. I usually have my preliminary studies pinned to the walls of my studio for the duration of a project, as a constant reminder of what I was "getting at" in the first place.

There also is a wonderful, embryonic vagueness in sketches. In their roughest form, loose scribbles suggest unintended objects, gestures, and facial expressions, any of which might be usefully elaborated. Sometimes I will also cut up and rearrange drawings with scissors and tape, which can awaken further "accidental" concepts. Most of the time I'm just keen to see what something looks like, and it doesn't have to be a good drawing. Paradoxically, I think that's exactly the frame of mind required to draw well, a simple and unassuming curiosity.

sketch for 'Eric'

38

study for The Rabbits : tree kangaroos + rabbits

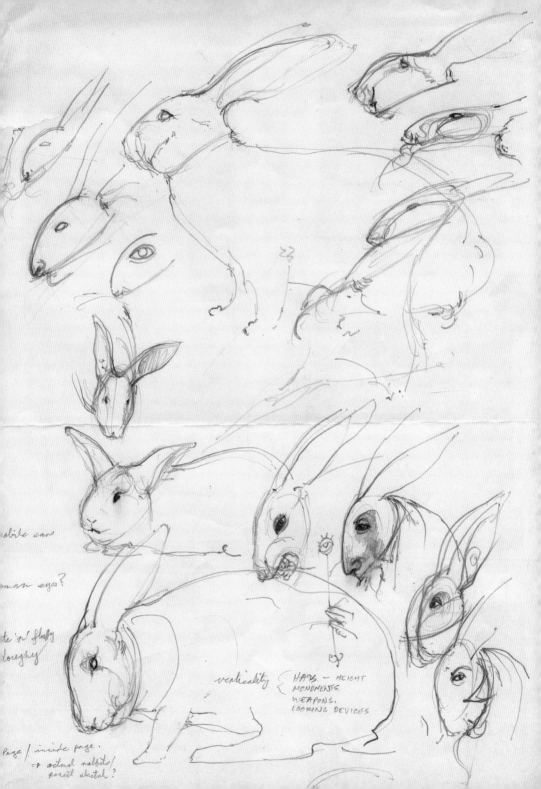

abile ears

man eyes?

te 'n' fluffy
doughey

verticality. { HATS. - HEIGHT
MONUMENTS.
WEAPONS.
LOOKING DEVICES

Page / inside page.
→ actual rabbits/
pencil sketch?

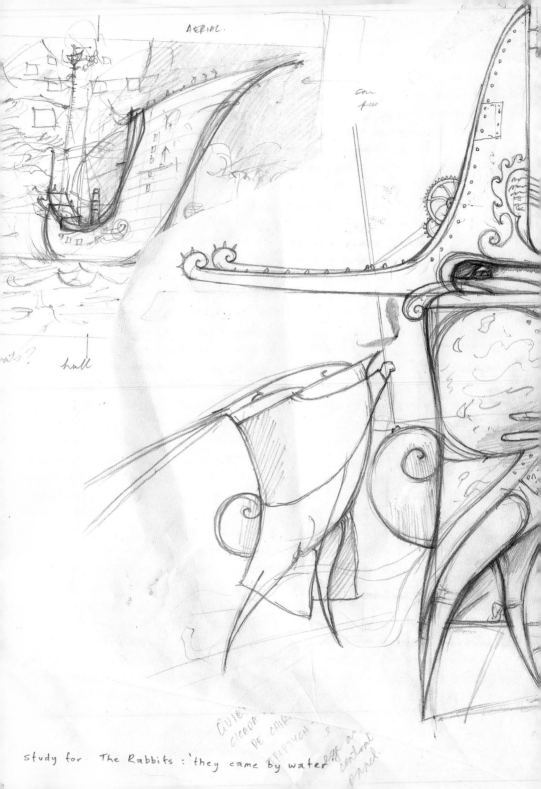

AERIAL.

can
fus

ats? hull

QUIE
CIENOP
DE CHIA

study for The Rabbits : 'they came by water'

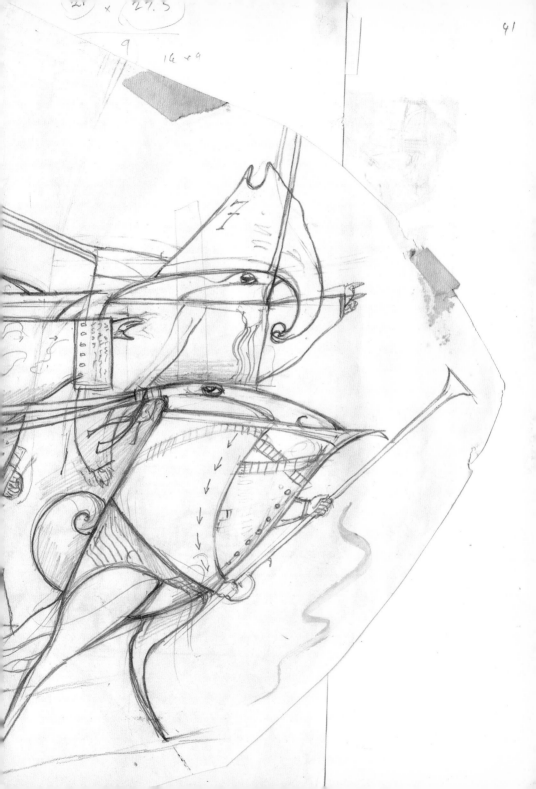

42

TAN.

studies for The Red Tree

44

It seemed friendly enough, though, once I introduced myself.

The Lost Thing - dummy page

I played with the thing for a while. Most of the day, actually. It was great fun. Yet I couldn't help feeling that something wasn't quite right.

As the hours slouched by, it seemed less and less likely that anybody was coming to take the thing home. There was no denying the unhappy truth of the situation: It was **lost**.

46

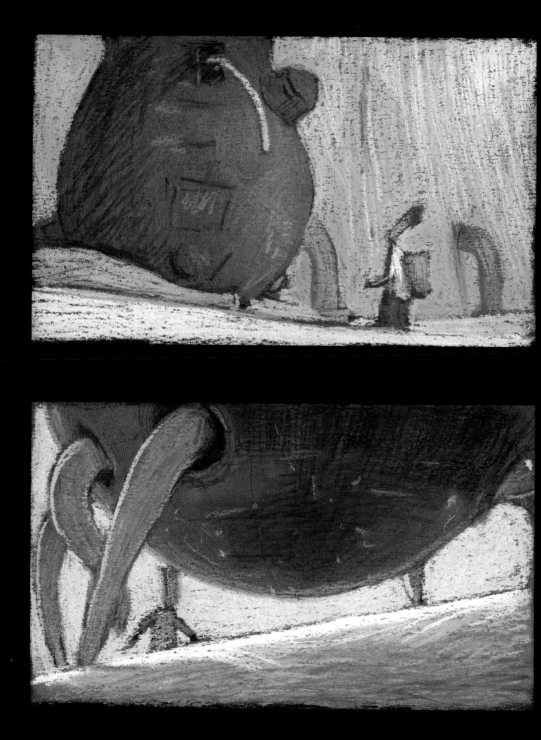

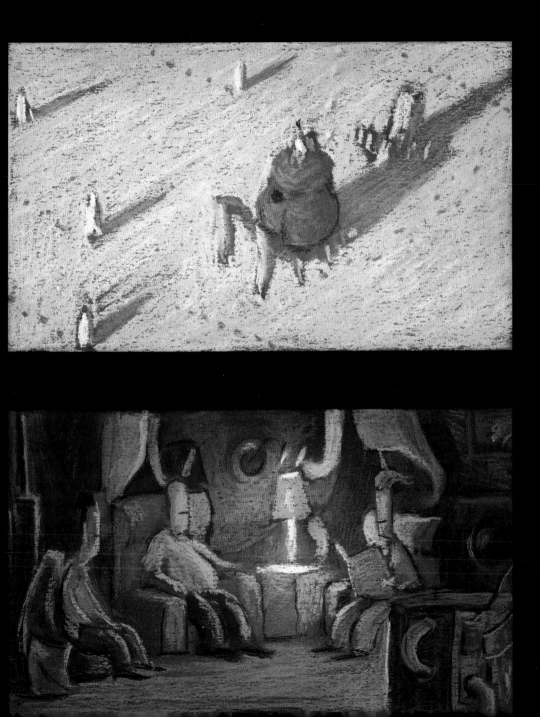

48

proud parents

cage-bird + obstetrician

object in a playground

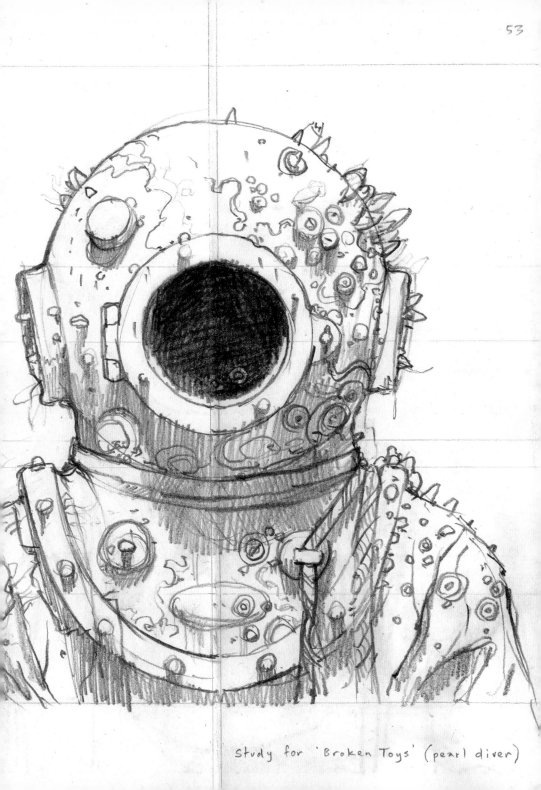

study for 'Broken Toys' (pearl diver)

54

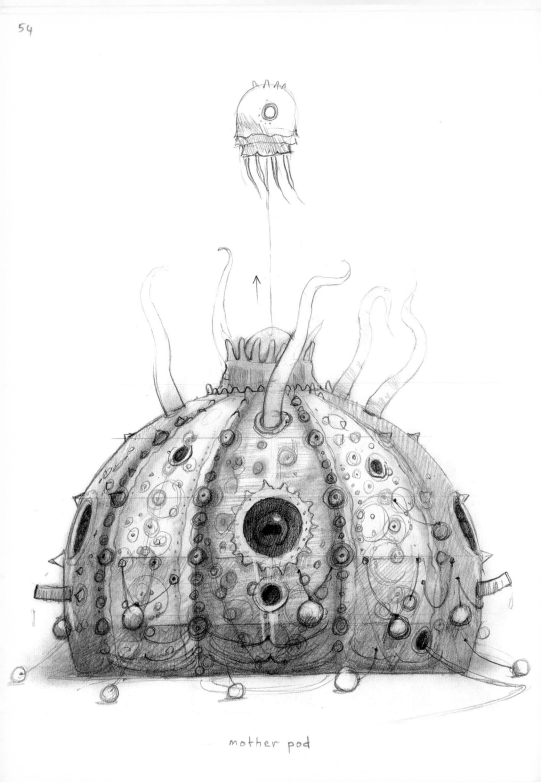

mother pod

terra-naut

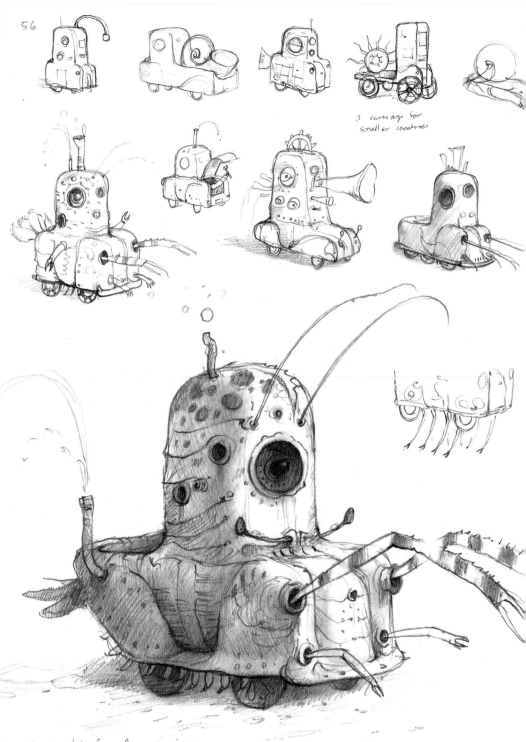

56

a carriage for
smaller creatures

concepts for Aquasapiens

SHRIMP CAR.

TAGS AROUND CITY.

DROPPING SMALL SEA SHELLS OCCASIONALLY.

I LOVE YOU

MERRY CHRISTMAS

ATTEMPTS TO COMMUNICATE

COMMUNICATING WITH EACH OTHER.

LURE WITH MONEY/OBJECT, MEASURE WITH TAPE

SHRIMP CAR MAKES ALL KINDS OF ANIMAL NOISES.
- DOLPHINS
- COWS
- DUCKS
- MACHINERY
- CAT MEOW.
- DOG BARKING

WIGGLING CLAWS/ TOUCHING CLAWS TOGETHER.

SHRIMP CAR FIXATING
ON CERTAIN 'LIKEABLE' INDIVIDUALS,
FOLLOWS THEM AROUND,
   TOUCHES THEM WITH FEELERS
→ SHRIMPY WANTS TO TOUCH
   PEOPLE ALL THE TIME!

PROBLEMS WITH STEPS, OTHER OBSTACLES, NOT BEING ABLE TO MOVE FORWARD.

HEY THERE LIL FELLA!

SHRIMPY BACKS OFF, EXPOSES CLAWS IF ANYONE GETS FRIENDLY BACK!

SHRIMPY FEEDING SEAGULLS, MAKING SEAGULL NOISES.

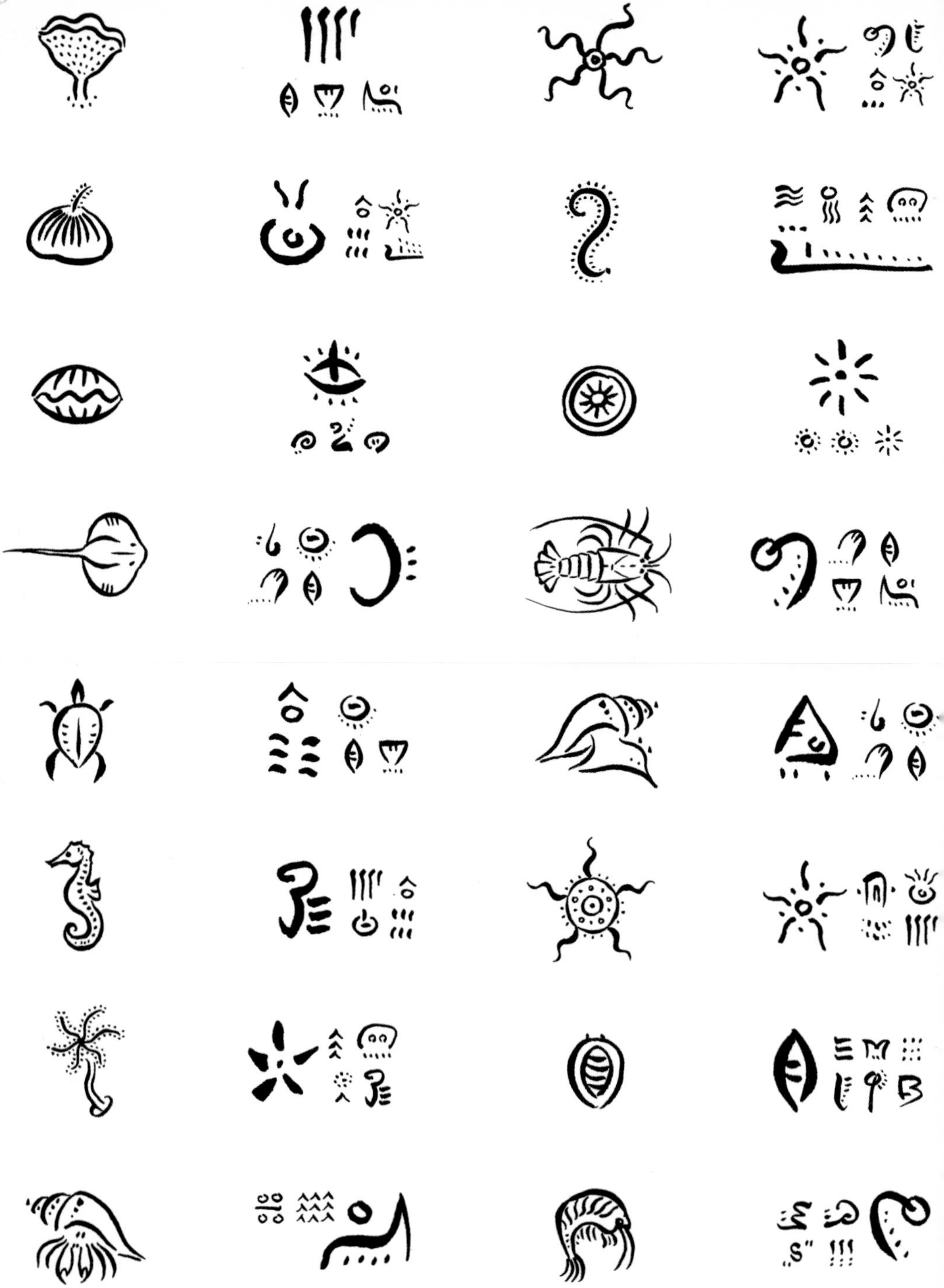

language of the sea

140°
130%

16 - 21.5

135%

'Tender Morsels'

8×10

23.52 — 290%
25.20 — 300%

200% to print
140%

sketch for 'The Arrival'

The Arrival · a game in the parklands.

65

storyboard for 'The Arrival: the night of the giants'

the water buffalo

FFEEEDIRP!

lizard - cat

drawings from life

Although a strong vein of fantasy runs through much of my work as an illustrator, its foundation lies in a careful study of the real world. In fact, there are few things I enjoy more than observational drawing, sketching the people, objects, animals, and places that are part of a more familiar, day-to-day reality.

A majority of my subjects are landscapes, which I find endlessly evocative as both abstract forms and conceptual maps. I'm especially interested in the tensions between natural and man-made forms, and this is a recurring theme in all of my paintings and stories. My drawings of people and animals relate to another abiding interest: the relationship between individuals and their respective environments, their sense of "belonging" to a place.

At a more elemental level, the sketches represented here are studies in the relationship of line, form, color, and light, where I'm trying to learn a vocabulary of visual ideas and skills that will inform all my other studio work. More importantly, I'm trying to develop a certain sensibility too, finding some emotional empathy with a subject, whether it is a person, a tree, or just a shadow on water.

Dad + me

study for a mural : 'the hundred year picnic'

SWEET.

DUSK HAZE.

CARNIVAL etc.

Simon + Guinness

18.5

162%
170%
190%
200%

Ryan

74

west coast highway

Very Sharp: hard-edge flat let forms,
    'hugged' by organic growth
    vertical indicators — repeating squares:
                              'suffocated' window

⊛ areas of special interest

    orange / white / green / yellow / grey-umber

                    sharp black points
    5:30   with rhyming diagonals

plus flat
grey & ochre
sky.

mawson crescent

Punji sleeping

78

coral tree, Bundanon

Mexico City

tuart tree

84

TREES IN A PADDOCK.

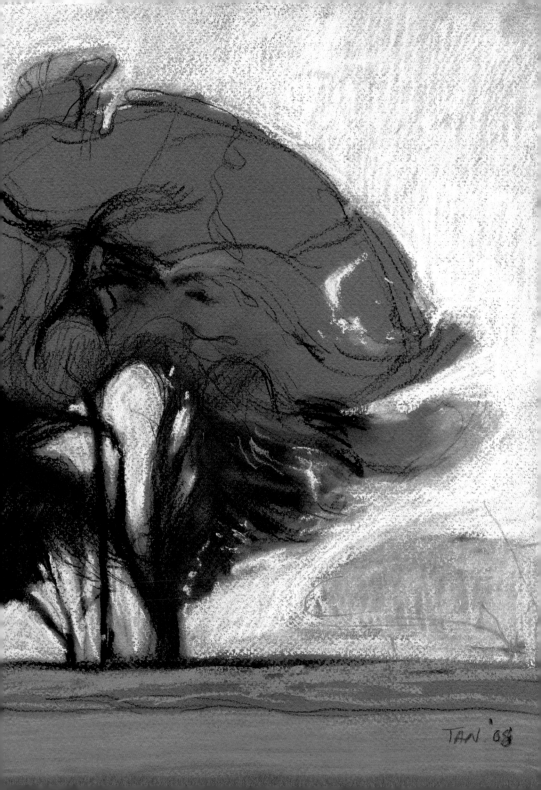

TAN '08

blue landscape

89

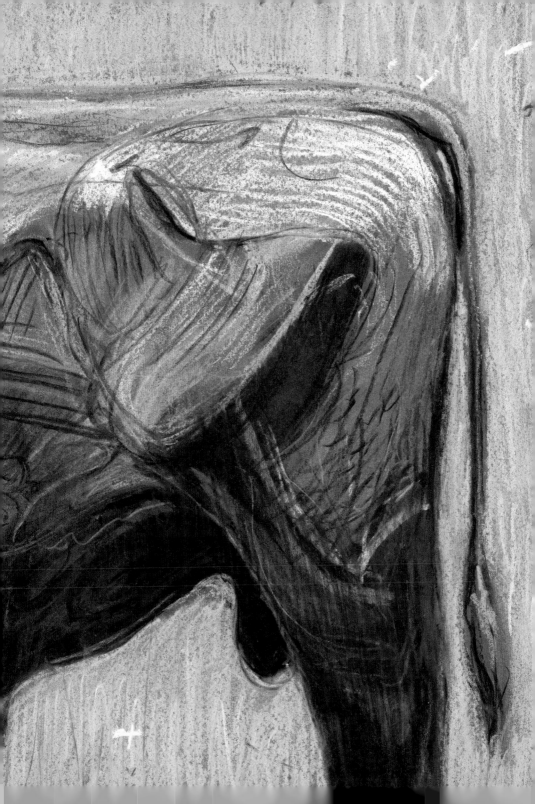

WET LANDSCAPE WITH NIGHT TRAIN

SILVER BLOOMS. DUBLIN MAY 09

notebooks

These are a set of sketchbooks that are quite small and easy
to carry around outside my studio, and most of the following
pages have been penned or penciled while traveling (often
in planes or trains). The best thing about them is their
lack of seriousness, generally using a cheap ballpoint pen
on average-quality paper, as if to remove any pretense of
"art." The resulting doodles are simple, unself-conscious
scribbles - ideal starting points for more considered
drawings. That said, I did have reservations about
including them in this book, as they are the antithesis of
"publishable" work to me: awkward, incoherent, and unedited.
But of course, that's the very thing that makes them
interesting, so here at least is a representative sample.

Some of these are observational, quick interpretations
of anything from museum objects to pictures in magazines.
Sketching things can help me to examine a fleeting interest
at a deeper level, taking a moment to pause and look. At the
same time, notebooks are there to jog my memory later on,
and if I don't jot down an idea, I'm most likely to lose it.

Other sketches are not observational at all, but an
equivalent to daydreaming: small thumbnail doodles that
open a passage between waking and subconscious concerns.
This always reminds me of fishing - casting loose lines
into a random sea, trying to hook something substantial.
It's surprising what sense can emerge from nonsense, and
how the juxtaposition of odd images on a page can have a
serendipitous effect, catching ideas that might otherwise
be hidden beneath the waves.

ELEMENTS ANTICIPATED.

HOW IT GOES.

NOBODY ELSE WOULD UNDERSTAND.

THE WAITING VILLAGE

WATCH TOWER

THE LONELY TOWER

CRASHED SATELLITE

BROKEN BODIES.
IMPERFECT.

BRICK?

EFFIGIES

GARDEN
WOOD SLATS.

HEDGEROWS
OR POPLAR
WALL

BIRDS.
MAGNUM
308

GEESE

DOORS?

SCARECROWS

+ VEGETABLE
GARDEN

CHECK
NELSON
PKS.

A WORLD OUT OF CONTROL

FULL CIRCLE
RAINBOW + OTHER
BLUE SKY EVENTS

MIDNIGHT
MASKS. IN
THE MAD CITY

BILLBOARDS
+ PICTURES

STUART FRANKLIN
'THE TIME OF TREES'
'THE DYNAMIC CITY'

THINGS DAD DID.

102

THE HOUSE

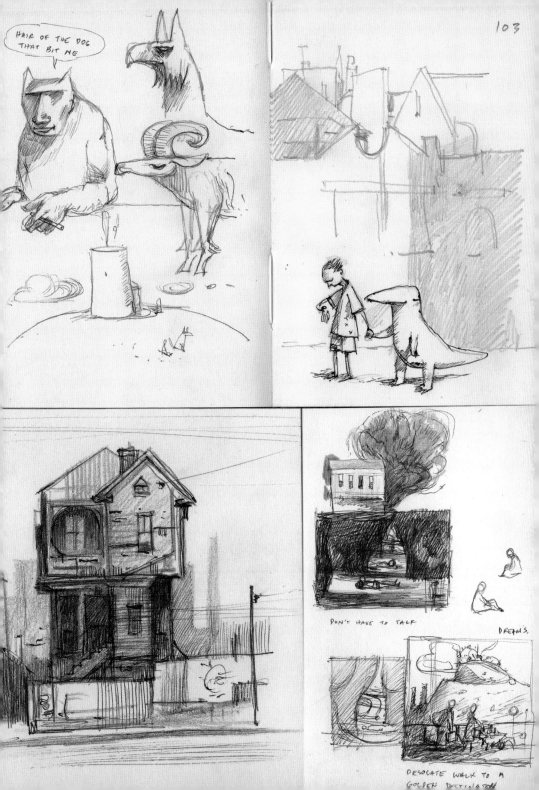

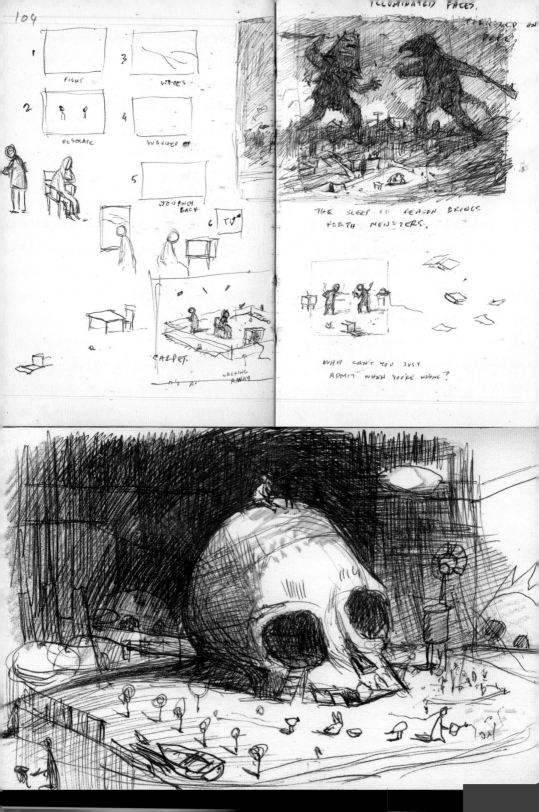

1 FIGHT
3 WAVES
2 DESOLATE
4 WASHED UP
5 JOURNEY BACK
6 TV

CARPET.

LOOKING AWAY

ILLUMINATED FACES.

THE SLEEP OF REASON BRINGS FORTH MONSTERS.

WHY CAN'T YOU JUST ADMIT WHEN YOU'RE WRONG?

- HE STILL HAD HIS HAIR,
  NEATLY COMBED.

- WHEN HE SLEPT, THERE
  WAS A SMALL VILLAGE IN
  HIS EYE SOCKET.

WIRE →

WHAT'S IN
THE BAG?

THE BOY WITH A SEWN-ON CAT HEAD.

- A TERRIBLE ACCIDENT THAT NOBODY
WANTED TO TALK ABOUT, IN A COUNTRY NO
ONE KNEW THE NAME OF. TERRORISED AT
SCHOOL, ALWAYS DRAGGING A BAG OF
SOMETHING.
WE WERE TOLD NOT TO PLAY WITH HIM.
SO WE DIDN'T.

THE MAN WHO WAS ALREADY A SKELETON.

- HE WENT TO THE SHOPS EVERYDAY, BUT WHAT
WOULD HE NEED? LAUNDRY SOAP... WOULD HE
REALLY GET THAT DIRTY? (HE SEEMED
SCRUFFY, BUT NEAT + CLEAN, AS IF SEEING
THE ORDER OF BONES HELPED.). HE BOUGHT
CIGARETTES BUT NEVER SMOKED THEM, JUST
PUT THEM IN THE FRIDGE. HE BOUGHT FOOD
LIKE FLOWERS TO WATCH THE RICH COLOURS,
THE REMINDER OF PASSING DELIGHT, UNTIL THEY
ROTTED AND HE BURIED THEM IN THE GARDEN.

WINDING ROAD

Pre-Columbian Pottery
Museo Nacional de Antropologica,
Mexico City

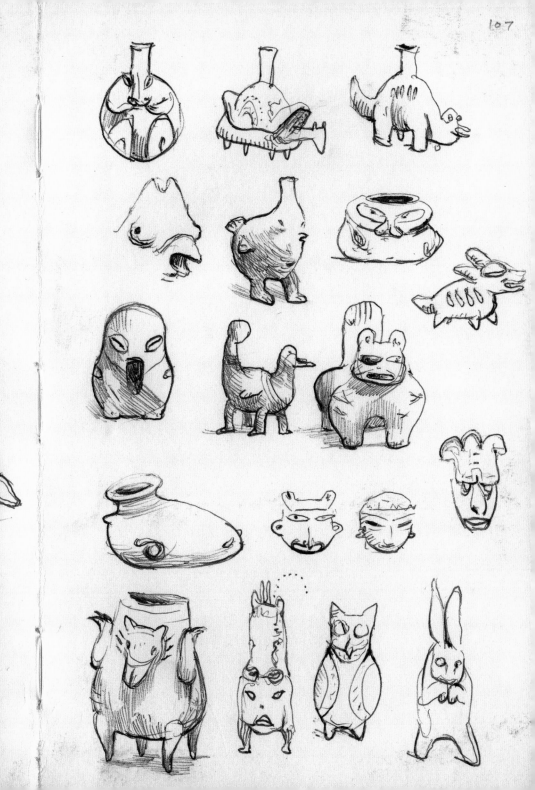

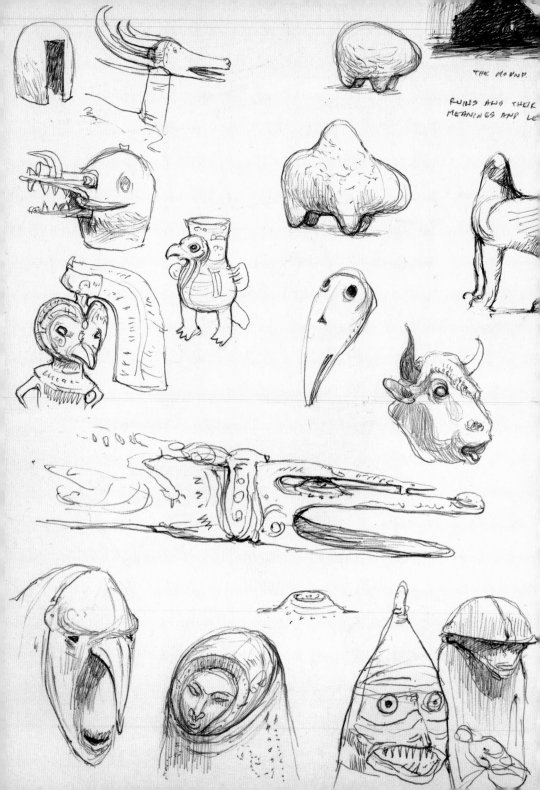

109

Sketches from
The Met, New York

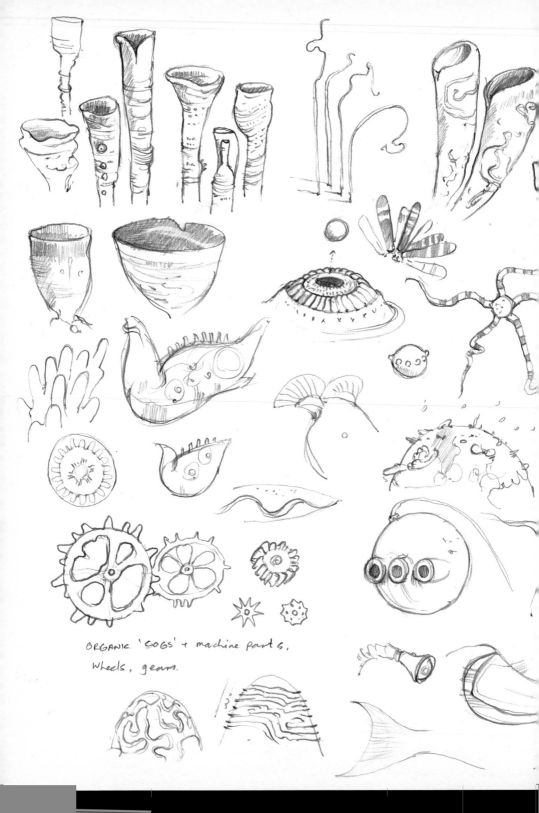

ORGANIC 'COGS' + machine parts.
Wheels, gears.

SOFT, TRANSPARENT

small sea life

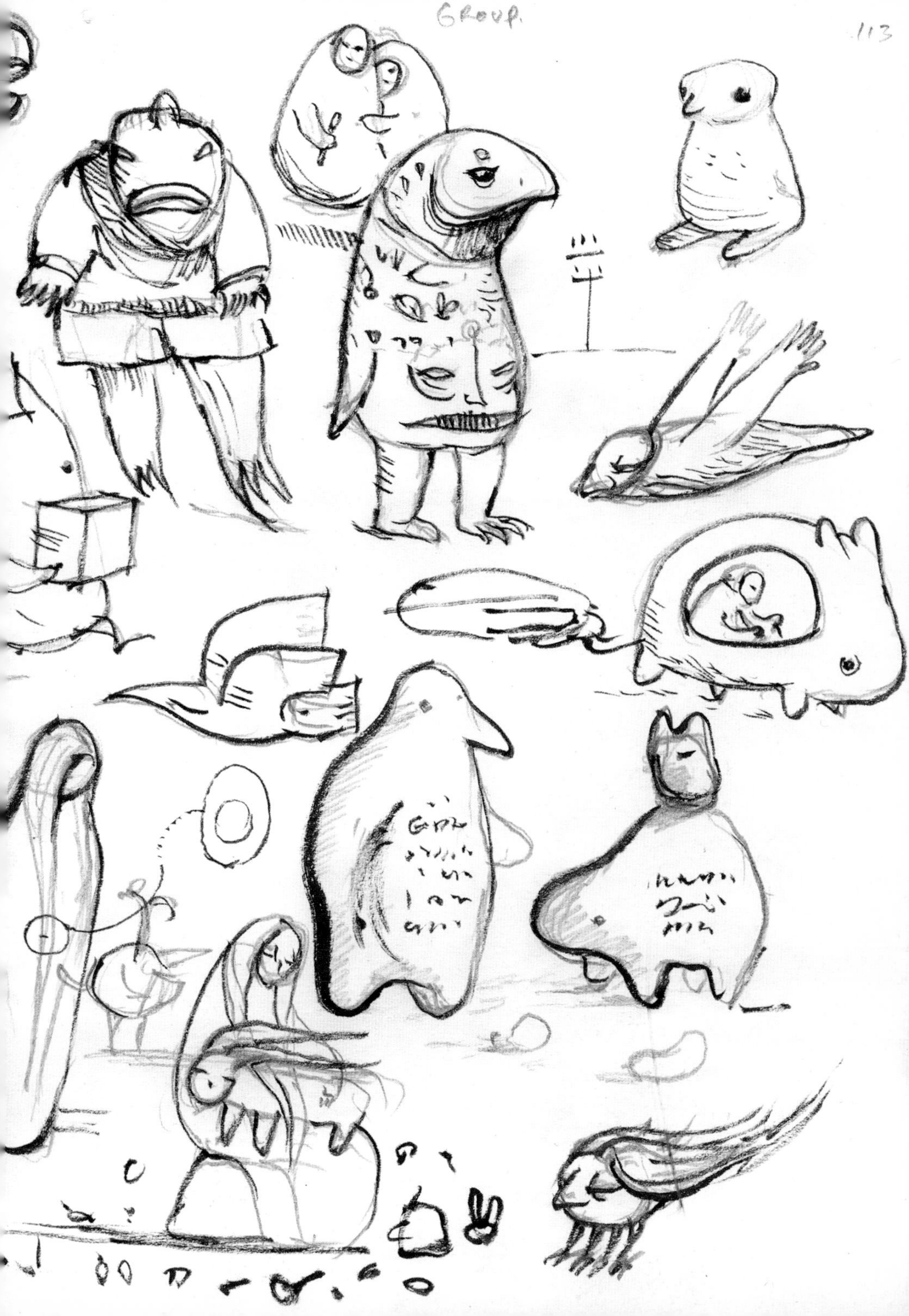
GROUP

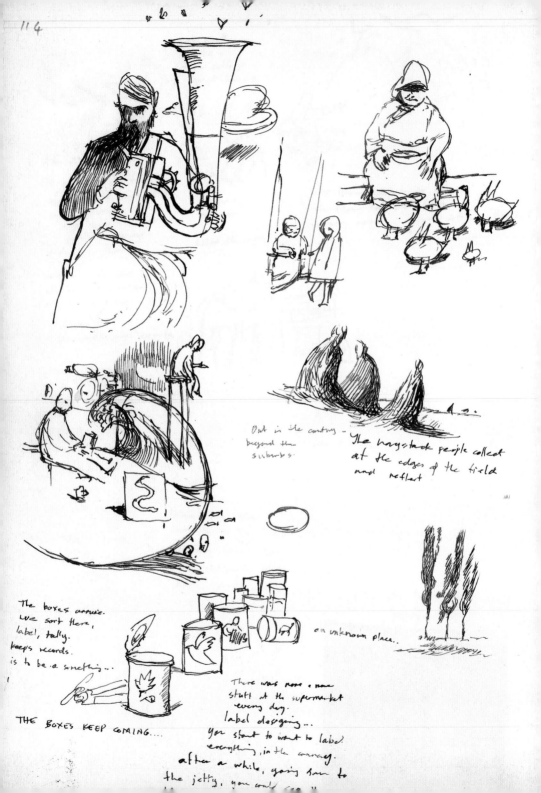

Out in the country —
beyond the
suburbs.

The haystack people collect
at the edges of the field
and reflect

The boxes arrive.
We sort them,
label, tally.
keeps records.
is to be a something...

on unknown place..

THE BOXES KEEP COMING....

There was more & more
stuff at the supermarket
every day.
label designing...
You start to want to label
everything in the cannery.
after a while, going down to
the jetty, you could see

I WOKE UP.
I DIDN'T KNOW
WHERE I WAS.

THERE WAS
A BAG,
MAYBE MINE

A VOICE.
SOMEONE
SAYING
WE HAVE
TO LEAVE.

AND THEY
RAN.

I TOOK
THE BAG
+ FOLLOWED

DOWN
CORRIDORS,

PAST STRANGE
THINGS, LIKE
PROPS. DO
I KNOW THEM?

WHERE
ARE WE
GOING?
NO ANSWER.

THEN A
SMALL
HOUSE IN
A PARK.
A TINY
DOOR.
ALL AROUND,
CUT DOWN
TREES

INSIDE,
MY PARENTS'
LOUNGEROOM,
ODD PICTURES
ON THE WALL

I LOOK CLOSE;
PICTURES OF
CATS I
DON'T KNOW.

THE PERSON
AGAIN, A
SMALL
CHILD; LED
ME UPSTAIRS

IN THE DESK,
DRAWINGS.

I REMEMBER
THE BAG,
FULL OF CRAYONS

↓

ABANDONED
QUARTER

A POINTLESS STRUCTURE

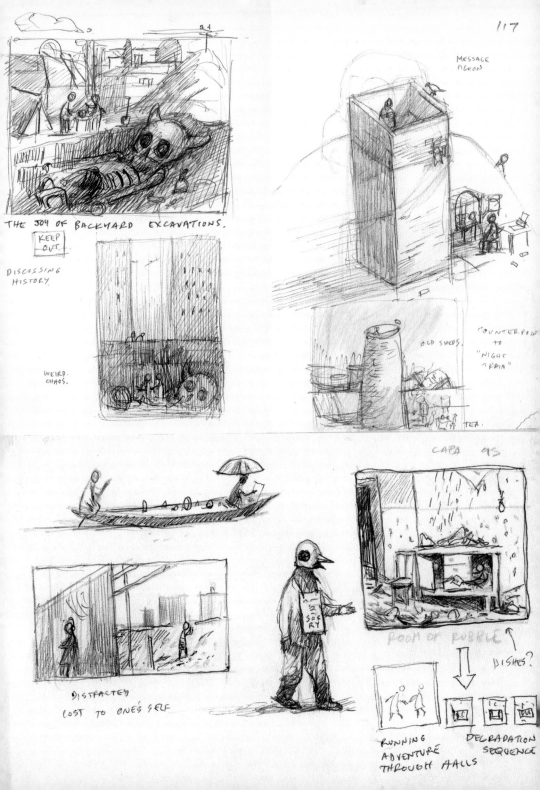

THE JOY OF BACKYARD EXCAVATIONS.

KEEP OUT.

DISCUSSING HISTORY.

WEIRD. CHAOS.

MESSAGE PIGEON

COUNTERPOINT to "NIGHT TRAIN"

OLD SHEDS.

TEA.

CARD 95

ROOM OF RUBBLE

DISHES?

DISTRACTED

LOST TO ONE'S SELF

I'M SORRY

RUNNING ADVENTURE THROUGH HALLS

DEGRADATION SEQUENCE

OUR HOUSE FAR AWAY.

WHAT A SORROWFUL
THING IT WAS, HAUNTING
THE EMPTY ~~ISLES~~, SUPERMARKET AISLES:
STUDDED WITH OLD JAM
JARS, ~~WITH~~ THE LABELS
REMOVED --- SMALL EYES
LOOKING OUT THROUGH~~OUT~~ THE
BOTTOM.

121

ADMIN.

INVENTED FESTIVALS.

COIN RETURN

NEITHER HERE NOR THERE.

GIANT WREN

LOW CONTRAST CLOUDS

THE TROUBLES OF

NOW IN PAPER- BACK

HORSE-GIRL

DERAILED TRAM.

FEAR #.6

GREED

SISTERS.

LAUNDRY.

- PENANCE

~~WAKING~~
⊞ WAKING

GUIDANCE.

▣ DEATH.

TALK IT OVER IN THE BIRD ROOM.

list of works

Title Pages

1 **Guardian**, *pencil*.

2–3 **The eight eggs (the bird king)**, *graphite and colored pencil*.

Untold Stories

7 **Bee-eater**, *pencil*. One of a series of unpublished drawings of homemade pets.

8 **Tea ceremony**, *pencil*. Concept sketch for an undeveloped picture book.

9 **Summoning**, *pastel crayon*. A sketch for a comics anthology on the theme "flinch."

10 **Anthropologists**, *pencil*. One of the drawings that best exemplifies my interest in foreign visitors and cross-cultural communications.

11 **Automatic teller**, *pencil*. An early concept sketch related to the picture book *The Lost Thing*.

12 **Astro-artist**, *pen and colored pencil*. Sketch to promote a children's art award.

13 **Furnace**, *pencil*. Concept for a Children's Book Week poster.

14–15 **Neighborhood watch**, *charcoal and pastel*.

16 **Boar**, *pencil & old architectural plans*. From the "homemade pets" series.

17 **Penguin**, *pencil & old architectural plans*.

18 **The water woman**, *pencil*. A drawing on the theme of regret.

19 **The thing in the bathroom**, *colored pencil*. Something to do with a rescued "puddle person."

20 **Self-awareness**, *pencil*. One of several drawings attempting to illustrate different attributes.

21 **Strawberry (contentment)**, *ballpoint pen*.

22 **Ancient ones**, *pencil*.

23 **Genesis**, *pencil*.

24 **Heart bell (the letter)**, *pastel and pencil*.

25 **Never lost a case**, *pastel and charcoal*.

26 **Best friends**, *pencil, digital*. Also related to *The Lost Thing*.

27 **Owl ghost**, *acrylic, oils, and collage*.

28–9 **Reading**, *graphite and colored pencil*. A sketch for a Children's Book Week poster.

30 **Tai chi master**, *pencil and ink*. Concept sketches for an undeveloped story.

31 **Philbert**, *ink*. An all-knowing character from an abandoned book project.

32 **Red donkey**, *acrylic*. A painting inspired by accidental brushmarks on scrap cardboard.

33 **Summit**, *pastel crayon*. A sketch inspired by a hill in New Zealand.

34–5 **Portrait of the artist as a young man**, *pencil*. Another poster for a children's art award.

Book, theater, and film

37 **Eric asks a question**, *pencil*. Preliminary sketch for the book *Tales from Outer Suburbia*. This story is about a peculiar foreign-exchange student.

38 **Tree kangaroos**, *pencil and felt-tip pen*. Drawings from Perth Zoo of marsupials from Papua New Guinea, which became the basis for the native "numbat" characters in *The Rabbits*, a picture book written by John Marsden. When creating fictional creatures, I almost always start by studying a real animal.

39 **Rabbit sketches**, *pencil*. The early evolution of a creature design, toward the stylized colonial protagonists of *The Rabbits*.

40–1 **They came by water**, *pencil*. A preliminary sketch for a key scene in *The Rabbits*, based on a famous Australian painting by E. Phillips Fox, *The Landing of Captain Cook at Botany Bay* (1902). A preliminary design for the grandiose "rabbit ship" is visible in the top left.

42–3 **Dawn and Bedroom tree**, *oil on board, pencil*. Preliminary sketches for *The Red Tree*, a series of paintings about depression and recovery.

44–5 **Saying hello and playing on the beach**, *pencil, photocopy, tape*. Pages from a dummy of the book *The Lost Thing*, the story of an unwanted animal lost in a bureaucratic city. Here I've worked out the arrangement of image and text using separate elements on detachable pieces of paper.

46–7 *The Lost Thing* film color script, *pastel on gray paper*. Some of the many preproduction drawings produced for a short animated film, an adaptation of the book. These color scripts served as a guide for the final lighting design of key scenes.

48 Proud parents, *pencil*. A concept sketch for *The Lost Thing* film, later modeled as three-dimensional digital characters in a "lost thing" paradise.

49 Cage-bird and obstetrician, *pencil*. More characters for *The Lost Thing* film.

50–1 Allegory of a family, *pencil*. A layout sketch for *Tales from Outer Suburbia*, about an imaginary mural discovered by an immigrant family in a secret room, accessible only through the ceiling space of their home.

52 Playground object, *pencil*. From a series of drawings of local suburban parks.

53 Pearl diver, *pencil*. A sketch of a mysterious character that appears in *Tales from Outer Suburbia*.

54 Mother pod, *pencil*. A concept drawing for the street-theater event *Aquasapiens*, commissioned by Spare Parts Puppet Theatre, Perth (2005). The central idea involved sea creatures that had developed a rudimentary technology to explore the "oversea" world – and human cities. Large-scale puppets moved through a central mall, interacting with people using claws, tentacles, water squirts, and sonic devices; also "tagging" unsuspecting specimens, by attaching strange symbols to their clothing.

55 Terra-naut, *pencil*. Another design for an *Aquasapiens* puppet standing about 4 meters high. One idea was that they might try to disguise themselves as humans in order to get closer to their research subjects.

56 Shrimp car, *pencil*. Designs for a crustacean that "mimics" a car, allowing it to surreptitiously collect any objects from the street that may be of scientific interest.

57 Aquasapien concepts, *pencil*. Behavioral ideas for the *Aquasapiens* project. Each creature was operated by a fully concealed puppeteer.

58–9 Language of the sea, *ink on paper*, *digital*. An imaginary alphabet used by the Aquasapiens to communicate their concerns. The hieroglyphs were printed onto business cards and handed out to people in the street.

60 Polar bear and demon, *pencil*. A sketch for the cover of the novel *Crusader* by Sara Douglass.

61 Tender morsels, *pencil*. A sketch for the cover of the novel *Tender Morsels* by Margo Lanagan.

62 Shadow, *pencil*. A preliminary study for the graphic novel *The Arrival*, a wordless story of immigration. Here, a poor family walks through the streets of the crumbling "Old Country," while mysterious black serpent-forms drift overhead.

63 Parklands, *pencil*. A preliminary sketch for *The Arrival*, exploring the strange natural beauty of the nameless "New Country." I had the idea that figures in the foreground would be playing an exotic bowling game.

64–5 The night of the giants, *pencil*. Pages from a dummy for *The Arrival*, describing a refugee couple's escape from genocidal beings, a metaphor for various 20th century atrocities.

66 The water buffalo, *pencil*. A drawing that inspired the opening story of *Tales from Outer Suburbia*, about a wise animal that never speaks.

67 Lizard cat, *ballpoint pen*. Concepts for a pet creature in *The Arrival*.

Drawings from life

69 Dad & me, *acrylic and pencil*. A painting based on an old family photograph.

70–1 The hundred-year picnic, *acrylic and oils on paper*. A preliminary painting for a large-scale mural at the Evelyn H. Parker Library in Subiaco, Western Australia, based on a local historical photograph.

72 Simon & Guinness, *acrylic on photocopy*. A study for a portrait of a friend, his dog, his rally car, and favorite beverage.

73 Ryan, *pencil*. Another study for a portrait of a friend, one of several drawings representing different moods.

74 West coast highway, *pencil*. A very familiar section of main road in the Perth suburb of North Beach, between my home and the city.

bibliography

Illustrated books
Lost & Found: Three by Shaun Tan, Arthur A. Levine Books, New York, 2011
Tales from Outer Suburbia, Arthur A. Levine Books, New York, 2009
The Arrival, Arthur A. Levine Books, New York, 2007
Memorial (written by Gary Crew), Lothian, Melbourne, 1999
The Viewer (written by Gary Crew), Lothian, Melbourne, 1997

Film
The Lost Thing, Passion Pictures Australia, 2010, director
WALL-E, Pixar Animation Studios, 2008, concept artist
Horton Hears a Who, Blue Sky Studios, 2008, concept artist

Theater and stage adaptations
The Arrival, Red Leap Theatre, Auckland, 2009
The Red Tree, Australian Chamber Orchestra, Sydney, 2008
The Arrival, Spare Parts Puppet Theatre, Perth, 2006
Aquasapiens, Spare Parts Puppet Theatre, Perth, 2005
The Lost Thing, Jigsaw Theatre Company, Canberra, 2004
The Red Tree, Queensland Performing Arts Centre, Brisbane, 2004

thanks

to Mitch, Helen, Tina, Filomena, Will, Sophie, Julia,
Inari, Mum & Dad;

also to Arthur A. Levine Books and Scholastic, Allen &
Unwin, the Australian Society of Authors, Bundanon Trust,
the Children's Book Council of Australia, Children's Books
Ireland, Conaculta Mexico, Lothian/Hachette Australia,
Passion Pictures, Spare Parts Puppet Theatre, Subiaco
Library, and Toppan Leefung Printing.